Gay H Naramore

Queen Loo and Other Poems

Gay H Naramore

Queen Loo and Other Poems

ISBN/EAN: 9783337325299

Printed in Europe, USA, Canada, Australia, Japan

Cover: Foto ©Thomas Meinert / pixelio.de

More available books at **www.hansebooks.com**

EN LOO,

AND

R POEMS.

BY

PHILADELPHIA:
J. B. LIPPINCOTT & CO.
1873.

Entered, according to Act of Congress, in the year 1873, by
GAY NARAMORE,
In the Office of the Librarian of Congress at Washington.

LIPPINCOTT'S PRESS,
PHILADELPHIA.

CONTENTS.

	PAGE
QUEEN LOO, THE PREHISTORIC WOMAN	5
RIGHTS AND WRONGS	23
MARIAMMIE	40
BEER AT EBB	45
"WELL CONTENT"	47
THEN AND NOW	48
LOUISE	49
THE POET	51
THE SHORELESS SEA	53
EVELYN	55
BE FAIR	57
NO, OH, NO	59
MY VALENTINE	61

CONTENTS.

	PAGE
FOR A DAY	62
A DREAM	64
NIGHT	65
ALONE	67
THE LAND OF SLEEP	71
GAINS FROM LOSSES	74
THESE SUMMER NIGHTS	78
HOPE AND DESPAIR	80

QUEEN LOO,

THE PREHISTORIC WOMAN.

I.

THE Assyrians, an old nation,
Have a legend of creation
Somewhat different from ours,—
Which says men grew first like flowers
From the bosom of the earth,
Nourished by sun, dew, and mirth
Of the winds and spirits airy,
Which rule over the realms fairy,
Till their childhood chrysalis season
Passed,—when gaining sense and reason,

They were first allowed to walk,
Wonder, wish, laugh, weep, and talk,
Hoard up gems and wager odds of them,
Fancying wealth would soon make gods of
    them.

II.

In those days the women were
Rare as well as very fair.
They were not seen in all doors
Then (as now) by threes and fours
Up to dozens and even scores,—
For the women were Kohinoors
In those days! They only grew
Shady as wild lilies do.
Under battlemented walls
Of mountains they sang madrigals,—

Hid they in Titanic alleys,

In the deeps of wooded valleys,—

Quiet grew they, not like chicken-sons,

Woodhull-Claflins, nor yet Dickensons!

III.

Tim-mer-lo was the first man,

So the ancient legend ran,

To fulfill the laws of fate,

And arrive at man's estate.

Tim-mer traveled far and wide

And the olden world espied,

From the farthest Orient sea

To the wilds of Thessaly.

What a wondrous virginal world

Must have been to him unfurled!

He was doubtless edified,
Must have opened his eyes wide
To take in the monstrous stature,
Reach, and power of mother Nature;
For in those days great commotion
Mixed the air, earth, fire, and ocean,
Geysers spouted, earthquakes shook the earth,
Huge beasts roared, waxed great and took the earth.

IV.

Tim-mer-lo was the first human;
Loo-ai-lo, the first earth-woman,
Grew beside a beautiful stream,—
Life to her was a flowery dream,—
Lotus first and woman after,
Heart brimful of love and laughter,

Lips that lapsed from smiles to sighs,
Languishing dark twilight eyes,—
What do you think her feelings were
Looking first on that valley fair?
Beautiful birds and passion-flowers,
Fruits in purple and golden showers,
Plenty of gorgeous shows and sights,
But no man who had more rights!
Nightingales sang fresh songs unto her,
Mock-birds and gaudy joys would woo her,
Plenty of pets she was beset with,
But, alas! no man to coquet with!

V.

Pondering much and traveling slow
In these days was Tim-mer-lo.

Careless of self, little knowing
On what errand he was going,
Little dreamed he then of wooing,—
He was really interviewing
Nature, and from land to land
Seeking her laws to understand,—
First the plant and then the man
Darkly reasons out God's plan.

VI.

But anon doubts rise, for pray
Why should all the world be gay
With its kind save only man?
Why should he be under ban?
Was man placed in the universe
As a target for God to curse?

Thus did knowledge first perplex,

Torture, tantalize, and vex,

But could never quite destroy

Reason's great and supreme joy.

VII.

Loo-ai soon tired of a life

Passionless and void of strife.

Tim-mer found his powers too slow

For the finding out what he would know,

And the doing what he would do.

Countries named he on his way,

Those high plains of Tartary

He first called them Cambulay.

Named some fair lands from the sun,

And some others from the one

God, the moon and stars, and hours
He looked on them, and flowers
Which grew there. So he left Belfountain
And climbed over the Star Mountain,
And looked down on Lotus River
Flashing to the sea forever.

VIII.

Loo grew weary of day's brightness,
Of the river's silvery whiteness,
Of the nights so lone and long,
Of the nightingale's sad song,
Of the cuckoo's plaintive cry,
Of the mock-bird's minstrelsy.
She plucked fruits with idle hands,
Dreaming naught of Hymen's bands,—
Decked herself with scarlet flowers,
Dallying with the golden hours,—

Wondered if this life is all,—
Wondered if that mountain wall
Is the world's end, when behold,
In the twilight's paling gold,
O'er the heights in day's last glimmer,
Towers the manly form of Tim-mer.

IX.

There they met then face to face,
Manhood's strength and woman's grace,
And, alas! she looked with favor
On the form of her enslaver,
Egotistic haughty man,
The arch-tyrant, naughty man!

X.

That they met with kindly feeling
There is no use in concealing,

For the old Assyrian singer's
Fancy kindles, glows, and lingers
As the story he rehearses,
Through a hundred rhythmic verses,
Of the love of Tim and Loo,—
How like yet unlike the two!
How he, soon as he had found her,
Loved, adored, worshiped, crowned her!

XI.

Can such love die? Ask the sun
Where his rays go when day's done.
From the first Tim worshiped Loo,
(As, my darling, I did you!)
Not alone as a proud queen,
The One Fair the world had seen,

She was more,—this radiant She
Was to him divinity!
An incarnate spirit of Light,
Inspiration day and night,
Faith, Hope, Courage, and Delight!

XII.

Hence, to prove his deep devotion,
He ransacked the earth and ocean
To find treasures rich and rare
Enough for his Queen to wear.

Time sped on,—days, months, and years,
And as yet love had no fears.

The world flourished,—growth and birth
Peopled the rich fields of earth.

XIII.

Tim-mer's younger brothers, Rim-mer-lo,
Skim-mer, Shim-mer, Fim-mer, Grim-mer-lo,
Blim-mer, Brim-mer, Dim, and Sim-mer-lo,
Taking high rank in creation,
Each one founded a great nation,
All of whom owned Tim-mer king.
He, being rich in everything,
Built a city with high walls
By the charming Lotus Falls,
At the very well-loved place
Where he first looked on Loo's face,—
Built a Pleasure-Dome of Gold
Filled with treasures manifold,—
Gave Loo rare things beyond price,
Fine white elephants and mice,
Pictures Venus would have cried for,

Birds the fairies would have died for;
In short, everything she sighed for.

XIV.

Still Love knew no base alloy,
Still she was his only joy,
Till it chanced one fateful day
A revolt in Cambulay
Called him from his throne away.

When she knew that he would go
Loo-ai clung to Tim-mer-lo,
And her eyes were like the skies
When the vernal storms arise.

Parting was like death to him,
But his banners were scarce dim

On the eastern mountain heights
Ere she planned to claim her "rights"!

XV.

Sim-mer, younger of the clan,
Fought the king at Cambulan,
Striving with his might and main
Separate kingship to maintain.

For a year the contest maddens,
All the land it curses, saddens,—
Finally at Lillipance
Sim-mer took a desperate chance,
Fought the king with all his forces,
And was rôuted, men and horses.
Peace was conquered, Sim-mer slain,
Tim-mer could go home again.

XVI.

During all this year no word
From the Queen had reached her lord;
For though men seem born good fighters,
Nature has no ready writers;
Neither was it thought the right thing
To send news express by lightning;
Hence the king, a happy man,
Hastened home from Cambulan.

XVII.

Left the battle-field and dying
And marched home with colors flying,
And forgot he was a foeman,
Dreaming dreams of a sweet woman
Who should greet him so and so—
Where he met her long ago.

Day and night o'er hill and plain

Hastening, scarcely drawing rein

Till he reaches Lotus Height;

When behold, now what a sight

Blinds his dazed and maddened eyes!

'Twas indeed a strange surprise,

Hell instead of Paradise!

XVIII.

Fancy his amazement when

A vast army met his ken,—

A huge army armed with spears,

With defiant yells and jeers,—

Rank on rank the countless hordes

Waved their spears and drew their swords,—

Thus beneath the twilight dim

Did his sweet Queen welcome him!

XIX.

For a moment his heart sank,

The world faded to a blank;

But anon his manhood came

And enlit his eyes with flame,

And his army charged that host

Reckless if they won or lost.

And they fought through all that night

By the wild moon's spectral light,—

And the king did win the fight.

Though the fair Queen was not slain

He ne'er looked on her again;

Never did he sigh or moan

More than if his heart were stone,—

And this was the King's decree:—

"THAT FOR ALL ETERNITY
HIS FAIR QUEEN SHOULD HAVE AND HOLD
HER PRISON-HOUSE, THE DOME OF GOLD."

This is all we can discover
Of Queen Loo-ai and her lover,
Who lived long and found life woe
Twenty thousand years ago!

RIGHTS AND WRONGS.

A MEDLEY.

I.

EVER since men dwelt on earth,
    Worn by care or cheered by mirth,
Labor has been crushed by rings
Of craven priests and cruel kings,
With each triple-guarded line,
Rights of might and rights divine.
Hence we see in History's pages
Naught recorded for long ages
But the story of the crimes
Of bad kings of evil times,—

How with gorgeous array
Ghengis Khan went forth to slay,
With such appetite for slaughter
That though blood flowed free as water
His mad passion was not cloyed
Till whole nations were destroyed.

II.

For long ages up and down,
Deified by priest and crown,
Conquest's Juggernaut passed on
Towards a goal it never won.

For innumerable years
Earth was cursed with blood and tears,
War and famine, desolation,
Night and hopeless lamentation;

But at last the morning broke,
And Hope's courage once more woke.

III.

Little heeded priests and kings
When the Mayflower spread her wings
To the free winds of the sea;
But on that day Tyranny
Got a blow which made it reel,
Got a wound which time can heal
Never. And as each day passes
Light shall reach earth's struggling masses
(Thanks to tongue and press and pen!)
Till all men shall know they are men.

IV.

Equal rights our fathers sighed for,
Worked for, fought for, lived for, died for,
And not vainly, but victorious,
For it was to them a glorious
And substantial consummation,
The firm-founding of a nation
Based on human brotherhood,
And the wisdom of the Good.

They would have men free to move,
Free to choose, live, do, and love,
Free to make in earth's waste places
Free homes for all creeds and races,—
With no class-rights to enslave us,
Free to speak the thoughts God gave us:

With such sublime theories
Did our fathers cross the seas.

V.

Brave old Pilgrims! What they bore
And forbore on sea and shore,
Toil, strife, famine,—dire distress
In a savage wilderness,—
Who can ever hope to tell?
Yet they passed the ordeal well,
For they triumphed over fate,
Many crookéd paths made straight,
And a thousand good deeds did
Which oblivion has hid.
Enough glory this alone
That they laid the corner-stone

For a Temple of the Free
Which should reach from sea to sea.

Inviolate thus far it stands
A hopeful beacon to all lands,
And if we build well as they
It shall not be for a day.

VI.

But the world moves on apace,
Steam and lightning take the place
Of the lumbering old stages,
While the Press crowds several ages
Into each one of its pages;
Steam and lightning, whiz and rush,
Put sweet nature's calm to blush,
Banish childhood from the earth,
Since there is no time for mirth

To hold holidays of gladness!

To get gold is the great madness.

All the grand ideal serenities,

All of art's divine amenities

Lost in wondering what will sell,

Sell and pay in traffic's hell!

VII.

And the demagogues from Tophet,

They too find confusion profit,

Like those men who with fine feeling

Follow fairs and fancy-stealing!

With their ignis-fatuus glamour,

And their hue and cry and clamor,

Would even sacrifice the Bible,

And make justice out a libel,

On a plea of equal statures,
Equal rights and equal natures,
Equal rats and mice and mousers,
Equal pockets, equal trousers!

VIII.

They talk parrot-talk by the hour
Just to get themselves in power,
And when this is nicely done
What do they care? Not a bun
If the whole world goes to smash,
So that they get lots of cash!

IX.

Our elections oft denote
Some men clearly live to vote;

While some pray, some curse by rote,

But your genuine mathematician

Settles every proposition,

Whether of heaven or hell's perdition,

Or the welfare of the nation,

With a meaningless equation,

As $a + b = y$.

Should you answer, If so, why?

He has nothing more to say,

Still his fallacy holds sway.

X.

And amid all this delusion,

Humbug-knavery, and confusion,

When the danger-signals flare,

And fierce tempests seize the air,

And our old experienced seamen

Lose their reckoning, why not women?

The curled darlings for whose pleasure
Men do sacrifice all leisure,
Wearing out their lives in toil
That no vulgar care shall soil
The delicate whiteness of their hands,—
They must war against Love's bands!
With their thin voice cracked with spites
They must needs shout "Equal Rights!"
They too have some waxen pinions,
They would soar to the sun's dominions!

XI.

Now, God bless them all! As mothers
They are equaled by no others,—
As the playful, dimpled sister,
Where's the man who has not kissed her?—
As the sweetheart she is fine,
Glowing, radiant, divine,—

And I yield my place to no man

In my love for the true woman.

Yet not less does her unreason

Look like blind and reckless treason.

XII.

Equal rights in property,

To be She as man is He,

We would grant her now, this minute,

And rejoice that she did win it.

XIII.

Still, we claim, her highest duty

Is to make home rich in beauty,

Love, and all the tender graces!

Oh, the dear, bewitching faces

Which we meet in strangest places!—

Yet we find, where'er we roam,
That man never has a home,
And cannot have anywhere
Without woman's love and care!

XIV.

Equal rights should mean far more
Than is known in modern lore,—
It sounds very well, no doubt,
And yet when you find it out,
'Tis an echo of no sound,
And is rarely on earth found;
Yet this shadow of a shade,
What huge conquests it has made!
Empires vaster it has won
Than the grand Napoleon.

XV.

'Tis a fast age without doubt,
Fast and past all finding out;
All we can is to surmise,
Dream and guess and theorize.
Should we answer with sage candor
Each malicious, pitiful slander,
We should waste our short-spanned life
Pandering to a fool's vain strife.

Let all those who choose go out
In the woods and scream and shout,
Call their enemies bad names,
And, consigning them to the flames,
Act like maniacs,—it is meet;
But in the populous city street

Mobs are dangerous disorders.

Freedom is not for marauders,

And the justice that is blindest

And severest is oft kindest!

XVI.

Let who will disown a Beecher

And make Train their moral teacher!

It would no doubt be quite legal

If we vote the crow and eagle

In all rights and choses equal,

But how would this change the sequel?

Long as lightning thrills the skies,

Long as love lights woman's eyes,

Long as love finds voice in words,

Eagles shall rule over birds.

Long as trees grow and winds sigh on
Shall earth's strong brute be the lion,
And while downward trends the water
Foolish lambs shall be for slaughter.

XVII.

What is the injustice, then?
Are men kept from being men?
Cannot seamen still be seamen?
And our helpmates still be women?
Who's compelled to shed his blood
For the right of doing good?
If we're powerful as a nation,
Must we, hence, defy creation,
And to prove it to the Hindoo
"Pitch our house out by the window"?

XVIII.

More fair than truth seem many lies,
But behold, the immaculate skies
Do not bend quite low enough
To embrace us in the rough,—
For at best we all are human,
Man is man, and woman, woman,—
And though some are angels nearly,
(And we love them very dearly!)
Many others turn out queerly,
And all "equals" this side heaven
Will not make the odd things even.
Yet while nations rise and fall
Nature's God reigns over all,
And all ages pass to prove
God's chief attribute is Love!

XIX.

After thunder-storm and wrack
Then come glowing, gushing back,
Clad in quaintest, daintiest ways,
Summer's perfect golden days.

Much is gold that we count dross,
Much is gain that we count loss:
After night and lamentation
Come the morn's transfiguration!

MARIAMMIE.

A TOUCHING BALLAD, SHOWING THE DANGER OF REFUSING A YOUNG MAN BECAUSE HE IS SMALL.

I.

BY the bottle-green Miami
    Dwelt a maiden with her mammy,
And her name was Mariammie,
And she loved a youth named Sammy,—
Little Sammy Himilay,
Of the town of Pickaway,
By the bottle-green Miami,
In the State of Ohi-o!

II.

But all this was years ago,
When the maiden was sixteen,
Full-grown, radiant, and serene
As a queen,
While the lad was small and green;
Greater contrast ne'er was seen:
Yet they loved each other so,—
Hence the woe!

III.

"Oh, my darling little Sammy!"
Sighed the maiden Mariammie
To herself.—"If you were taller,
Only by an inch or two,
You might do;

But to marry one so small
Would never do at all!"
And so,
Though
Her heart was full of woe
To refuse him,
And thus lose him,
Yet to all his wild entreaties
And love-ditties
She said "No,—
No, no, no!"

IV.

But that was years ago.
If she'd only told her reason
For refusing him, in season,
He had certainly grown bolder,

And had answered her, and told her

He would grow;

But, instead, he got unhappy,

And he went to Cincinnati,

And the maiden, with her mammy,

Listened to the sad Miami

All alone,—

Till her heart was changed to stone!

V.

But one day,

After years had come and gone,

Who should come to Pickaway,

Who, but Sammy?

"But, my stars, how he had grown!"

Said Mariammie.

"How could you so deceive me
And bereave me?"
Here she stared, and caught her breath,
And grew as pale as death,
For he—was not alone!

BEER AT EBB.

AFTER SWINBURNE'S "LOVE AT EBB."

I.

BETWEEN the seesaws of the sea,
    My friend laid hands and feet on me,
From beer-y gardens of delight
He kicked me forth into the night;
Ah, me, and what thing came so queer
Between the beer-foam and the beer?

II.

Between the sea-weed and the sea,
Grief ran to beer, beer ran to me,
Beer turned to fiends, and fiends to fire,
To burn me at my slow desire;

And then a Peeler did appear

Between the beer-foam and the beer.

III.

And as the sea-sand hugs the sea,

That Peeler watched one hour with me;

Then up the all-muddy stairs a flight

He went and swore that I was tight;

I saw him go and then draw near

Between the beer-foam and the beer.

IV.

Between the sea-salt and the sea,

Beer fell on sleep, sleep fell on me;

First star that rose saw beer, and I

One twain with beer between the sky;

The next that saw not me saw queer

Between the beer-foam and the beer.

"WELL CONTENT."

AFTER ALICE CARY.

ALL in the fair and freezing weather,
    Two gay children, John and Ann,
Slid down the Cambridge hills together,
    And slid the way their hand-sled ran.
The sun was low, not set, but pale,
And hectic as a comet's tail.

The clouds were driving swiftly o'er them,
    And their shadows on the snow
Moved swiftly on and on before them,
    As like an avalanche down they go,—
For they were lovers and well content,
Sliding the way their hand-sled went!

THEN AND NOW.

A THOUSAND years ago to-day
    Indians hunted up Broadway,
Hunted bear and deer with arrows,
Picked their bones and sucked the marrows,
Alas!

But now all is improved and changed
Since Red Men in the green-wood ranged,—
The bare and dear now hunt Broadway
For men with killing arts to slay,
A lass!

LOUISE.

SITTING by a summer sea,
    Listening to a melody
Which was old before the birth
Of man's prehistoric earth,—
Louise broke the magic spell
Which the waters weave so well.

And what would you think should please
A bright damsel like Louise?
A lover eloquent with lies,
Or poodle-dog with "glorious eyes"?
Alas, my friend, you do her wrong,—
She only asked me for a song.

And what less could the dear girl ask
Than just this trifling pleasure-task?
And who would not do more to please
And gain rich smiles from a Louise?
And who could ask more while Time's sea
Flows onward to eternity?

It is a little thing, a song,
But let no trifler do it wrong;
If the sweet singer have the will,
And love divine, and faith, and skill,
His song shall bloom when we are clay,—
The "blown dust" of a summer's day.

THE POET.

I.

THE world seems heartless, rough, and wild
 To the poet child.
And what is the poet?
A king on a throne
With infinite powers,
But with sceptre o'ergrown
And weighed down with flowers.

II.

THERE are forms of beauty,
And forms of light
That smile on the poet's soul from each cloud
That veils the beaming eyes of night,
While angels crowd
The tremulous air to whisper delight,—
And yet he always hears the moan
Of the sorrowful breeze
And desolate seas,
And his human heart is always lone.

THE SHORELESS SEA.

LIFE is a river
Flowing forever
Down to a boundless,
Fathomless sea.

From crystal fountains
Far up the mountains,
Through flowery ways
For a few fleet days
It laughs and plays,—
And then through many
A tangled maze!

God only knows,

Till death disclose,

What Fields Elysian,

What fair isles repose

In thy shoreless sea,

Eternity!

EVELYN.

A WILD-FLOWER maid with dimpled face,
   A charming frolic piece of human,
And yet in tender, soulful grace
   Where is there a more perfect woman?

She is as full of melodies
   As any song-bird of the meadows,
And who that once looks in her eyes
   Will e'er forget their lights and shadows?

Dark-brown hair with tints of gold
   A glorious lily brow adorning,

Enlit with smiles as rich as fold
    The ethereal form of morning.

And, oh! her voice is soft as dove's,
    When cooing all of spring-time blisses,
And lips such as Apollo loves
    To give his more than regal kisses.

A very child in form and face,
    A charming piece of frolic human,
And yet in tender, soulful grace
    Where is there a more perfect woman?

BE FAIR.

I HAVE loved you, we will say,
    All my life long, more each day,—
Still, we never have been wed,
Nor has any word been said
Until now, and now I say:
Kiss me not when I am dead,
But be fair, and kiss me when
I can kiss you back again.

You have loved me, we will say,
More each year, and month, and day;
Shall we wait till life be fled

BE FAIR.

Ere the word of words be said
Which our hearts so long to say?
Kiss me not when I am dead,
But be fair, and kiss me when
I can kiss you back again.

NO, OH, NO.

IT cannot be I love you. No,
    I never loved a woman. Yet
A something of you will not go
    When I would fain dream and forget,—
A something of your thought and air,
    A something of your lips and eyes,
Hovers around me everywhere,
    And fills my heart with vague surprise.

It cannot be I love you. No,
    For I was wedded to sweet art
So many, many years ago,—
    And yet my weak and foolish heart

Keeps picturing your image fair,
   Till for the smiles of your dear eyes
I would forego even Art's high care,
   And her divine amenities.

MY VALENTINE.

YOU thrill all my fancies
    By day and by night,
You I bless every morning
    And pray for each night,—
I think of you always,
    My life's one delight!

And you,—yes, I know it,—
    While life lights your eyes,
While the sun walks in glory
    God's star-inwrought skies,
You shall love me, shall love me,
    Whoever denies!

FOR A DAY.

MY sombre years have passed away,
    I have been happy—for a day,—
This shall console me if alone
I am compelled to journey on.

Say, do you know how many years
I loved you? Through what doubts and fears?
And have you now the heart to say,
Look not upon me from this day?

Yes, yes, I know. Our lives seem vain;
Smiling we drag an endless chain.
If it is fated that we part,
At least you would not break my heart.

FOR A DAY.

There is no loss without some gain,

And pleasure is not without pain.

Henceforth when heartsick I will say,

I have been happy—for a day!

A DREAM.

IN age we meet in hall and street
    A myriad forms that fade as fleet
As light-winged clouds,—and yet, and yet,
Whom we love first we ne'er forget.

We met in youth, when just to be
In this bright world was ecstasy,
When every feeling was in tune
With mirth, and song, and love, and June.

Birds sung, flowers bloomed, and all was gay,
For it was Love's own holiday,—
And each looked in the other's eyes
And dreamed a dream of Paradise.

NIGHT.

I.

YOU ask me what I love most
    Of God's works this side God,
The patriarchs of the forest
    Or the violets of the sod?
The boundless might of ocean,
    Or the mountain's sublime height?
The glory of the sunlight,
    Or the majesty of night?—
And I answer night, O night!

II.

For day is the slave of Mammon,
    And care is the goad that stings,

And the heart will not stop aching
   Whatever the robin sings;
And the boundless might of ocean
   Is a fearful and terrible might,
But night is a beautiful maiden
   Whose smiles fill our heart with delight,—
   And we love thee, beautiful night!

III.

Night with her witching shadows,
   Night with her gorgeous dreams
Which dwarf day's Eldorados,
   Though burning with golden beams,—
Night with her infinite fancies
   Sparkling with starry light,—
O night with thy wonderful glamour,
   I welcome thee, beautiful night,
   I love thee, heavenly night!

ALONE.

I.

THE regal moon looks proudly down
    Upon the gay streets of the town,
The stars are pale, the gas-light flares
In serried ranks along the squares,
While countless forms weird and unknown
Flow like phantoms up and down
Over the well-worn pavement stone,—
And while they pass and wax and wane
I sit with my cheek to the window-pane
Watching and waiting, and waiting in vain,
Alone!

II.

And what is it to be alone?

To feel no touch and hear no tone

Of kindred, and to meet no eyes

Thrilled with the thought which lights your own,

And yet to see,

As days drag by like weary centuries,

A wild immensity

Of frigid faces pass

Like shadows in a glass,—

This is to be alone.

III.

Alone in the crowded city,

Alas for the desolate years!

With a heart too wise for sighing,

Too wise and proud for tears.

In a crowd, and yet as lone

As though chained to a passionless stone,—

In a crowd with none to pity,

Or care for, or love, or hate,—

I am weary of such a fate,

I am sick unto death of the city

Where the hydra masses den,—

I will fly from the haunts of men.

IV.

Flow on proud, turbid river

To the sea that wails forever,—

I have listened all too long

The sad burden of your song.

V.

Afar are the purple mountains
Which have tantalized my sight
With vain longing day and night.
I will climb yon purple mountains,
And what then shall tempt me to roam?
I will follow the brooks to their fountains,
And find my long-lost home.
There hearts are true as the winds are free,
And there my mother will welcome me
To my own dear childhood home!

THE LAND OF SLEEP.

I.

I SOUGHT full long the land of Sleep,
   For I was wearied through and through
With toil which seemed good but proved vain,
And so wore out both heart and brain.
The winds through spice-bowers cooled with dew
Brought healing on their wings, and deep,
And beautiful, and dreamless sleep.

II.

I passed into the land of Sleep,
And all the world was left behind,—

The world of toil, and strife, and care,
And love, and heartache, and despair.
I felt again the gentle wind
Of childhood fold me,—soft and deep,
And full of heaven is childhood's sleep.

III.

I passed into the land of Sleep,
Where shadows hold high carnival,
And every voice is musical,
And all the powers of air and sea
Do minister to melody,
And no one ever cares to weep,
For none has time, so sweet is sleep.

IV.

I love the fairy-land of Sleep,
For there the doubts which vex the day

Are borne like summer clouds away,

And she, my one proud Queen of Song,

There never does me any wrong,

But loves me with a love as deep

As my heart craves,—thank God for Sleep!

GAINS FROM LOSSES.

I.

IN the busy Land of Moil,
   Where they make a God of toil,
And yield up their hearts of ice,
An ignoble sacrifice,—
In a city full of folks,
Who are but so many spokes
Of an ever-giddy wheel,—
There with all things did I reel.

Moiled I there day after day,
Day after day till old and gray,

Year after year, both soon and late,

As if driven along by fate,

Till my strength being overtasked,

"Wherefore?" finally I asked,—

"Wherefore all this blind turmoil,

Hopeless, heartless, slavish toil?

"Now I'll rest, or if I act,

Only keep my hoards intact;

From corruption, moth, and rust,

To keep safe my treasured dust,

I will build both strong and well."

But, alas! what citadel

Ever yet was strong to hold

That winged, sleepless demon, Gold?

II.

Long I strove with might and main
My lost treasure to regain,—
Yet, when certain it was gone
Past redemption, did I moan?
No, indeed not. Freed from care,
My heart felt as light as air.
Which were better, to be gay
Or the Emperor of Cathay?

And I left the city's din,
Babel, Babylon, dust, and sin,
And I climbed a mountain's crest
Which glowered dimly in the west,
And I looked down on a grand,
Virginal, wild, Promised Land,

Rich in fruits and flowers. Thus
I first saw how glorious

'Tis to dwell near Nature's heart,
Far from sullen crowds apart.
This crag-walled and sea-bound nook,
Which, they say, all else forsook,
Is my home,—and more my own
Than any king's his very throne,—
So loss proves gain as life's full days
Go by, unheeding blame or praise!

8

THESE SUMMER NIGHTS.

IN these quiet summer nights
   Which the moon more woos than lights,
When the stars lone vigils keep,
And the world is all asleep,
Just for the old dead love's sake
I am glad to be awake.

In a silent summer eve
Do you ever think to grieve
That we are so far apart?
For myself, I own my heart
Prayeth heaven unceasingly
That you may yet turn to me.

In such dreamy nights as this
Dreams are dreamed too full of bliss,—
Of listening to low replies,
While looking love in loving eyes,—
Alas, they are but mockery,
As my dreams ever seem to be.

In such quiet nights as these,
Even the hateful, dissonant seas
That divide us are at rest.
Oh, my old love, is it best
That I send o'er a wild sea
This poor song to plead for me?

HOPE AND DESPAIR.

PART I.

IN the mountain land of Hope
  How the rainbows beckoned onward!
How the golden vistas sunward
Brightened all our horoscope!

We had not a groveling thought,
  We would take no lowly station,
  Nature's bounteous inspiration
With what eagerness we sought.

Care we had not heard of then,
  And no Dragons ever daunted,

And no demon spirit haunted,
For we knew not doubt or pain.

Oh, those days! regal, sublime,
  When your high thoughts so up-raised me,
  And your glorious eyes so praised me,—
How could mortal choose but climb!

PART II.

But, alas! you passed Beyond,
  Dear Friend of prophetic vision.—
  While you roam in fields Elysian,
I am in the vale Despond.

And, alone, too well I know
  All the ordeal and the burden,

And the paltry, pitiful guerdon
Which adds bitterness to woe.

Love and Hope are both gone down,—
    All life's beauty, all life's glory,
    Fled beyond the mountains hoary,—
Where the rainbows were, the frown.

Through the lowlands of Despair
    Now I pass with trailing pinions
    To night's desolate dominions,—
And no gleam of hope is there!

www.ingramcontent.com/pod-product-compliance
Lightning Source LLC
Chambersburg PA
CBHW020326090426
42735CB00009B/1418